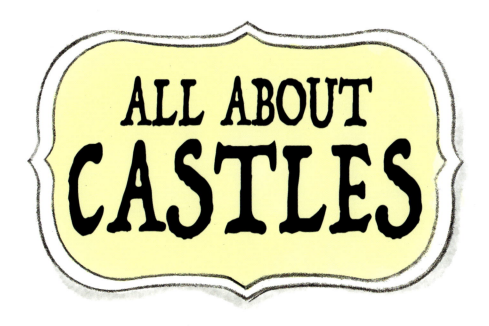

ALL ABOUT CASTLES

Written by Nell K. Duke, Douglas H. Clements, and Julie Sarama

Illustrated by Scott SanGiacomo

www.connect4learning.com

Copyright
©2016 Douglas H. Clements, Julie Sarama, Board of Trustees of Michigan State University, The Regents of the University of Michigan
Published by Connect4Learning®
An imprint of Gryphon House, Inc.
P. O. Box 10, Lewisville, NC 27023
800.638.0928; 877.638.7576 [fax]
Visit us on the web at www.gryphonhouse.com.

Reprinted June 2019

All rights reserved. No part of this publication may be reproduced or transmitted in any form or by any means, electronic or technical, including photocopy, recording, or any information storage or retrieval system, without prior written permission of the publisher.

The Connect4Learning® curriculum is based upon work supported by the National Science Foundation under Grant No. DRL-1313718. Any opinions, findings and conclusions or recommendations expressed in this material are those of the authors and do not necessarily reflect the views of the National Science Foundation.

Printed in the United States.

Cover and interior illustrations and design by Scott SanGiacomo.
Photography courtesy of Shutterstock Photography ©2016, www.shutterstock.com.

Library of Congress Cataloging-in-Publication Data

Names: Duke, Nell K., author. | Clements, Douglas H., author. | Sarama, Julie, author. | SanGiacomo, Scott, illustrator.
Title: All about castles / written by Nell Duke, Doug Clements, and Julie Sarama ; illustrated by Scott SanGiacomo.
Description: Lewisville, NC : Gryphon House, Inc., [2016] | Audience: Grade Pre-school, excluding K.
Identifiers: LCCN 2015036908 | ISBN 9780876596876
Subjects: LCSH: Castles--Juvenile literature.
Classification: LCC GT3550 .D85 2016 | DDC 392.3/6--dc23 LC record available at https://lccn.loc.gov/2015036908

Do you like houses with giant doors?

With hundreds of rooms?

With giant towers that seem to reach to the sky?

Then you like castles!

Castles are buildings that were built to protect the people who lived in them from attack.

Many castles were built for kings and queens.

People who worked for the king and queen sometimes lived in the castle too.

Many castles had features to help keep enemies out.

Many castles had guards to keep the king and queen safe from enemies.

Many castles had large rooms with fancy decorations and special chairs for the king and queen to sit in.

There are still castles today.

People visit castles.

Castles can have many different styles and features.

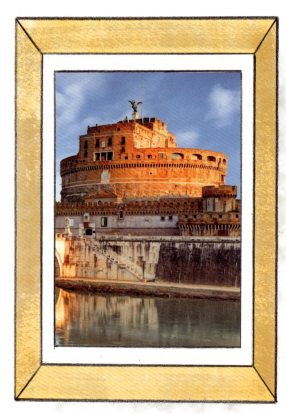

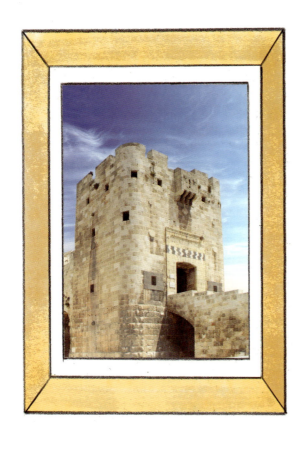

You can build your own castle in a variety of ways.
Let's try blocks.

You can use rectangular prisms to make the walls.
Why do you think they stack so well?

And you can use half-circles to make arches for the drawbridge.

Most castles are symmetric—that means they look exactly the same on one side as on the other.

If you run out of long rectangular prisms like these,

you can use four shorter ones like these.

For the towers, you can use cylinders with cones on the top.

Inside the castle walls, you can use triangular prisms to build a ramp. The ramp can get knights and heavy things such as catapults up to the top of the walls.

At the top of the walls, some castles have a pattern of stones carved in the shape of rectangular prisms and spaces that knights could peek out of.

Some castles have many other shapes of towers and roofs.

Castles are great fun to build with blocks. What features will you put in your castle?